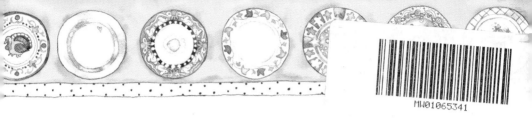

A Home Built With Love

DEBBIE KINGSTON BAKER

HARVEST HOUSE PUBLISHERS
Eugene, Oregon 97402

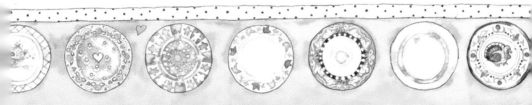

*Dedicated lovingly to Duane,
with whom I am so at home*

A Home Built with Love
Copyright © 1999 Harvest House Publishers
Eugene, Oregon 97402

ISBN 0-7369-0114-0

Artwork designs are reproduced under license from © Arts Uniq'®, Inc., Cookeville, TN and may not be reproduced without permission. For information regarding art prints featured in this book, please contact:

    Arts Uniq'
    P.O. Box 3085
    Cookeville, TN 38502
    800-223-5020

A portion of the artist's royalties from this book will go to benefit the National CASA Association. CASA volunteers all across the country work to find safe, permanent homes where abused and neglected children can thrive. For more information about CASA, please call (800) 628-3233.

Design and production by Garborg Design Works, Minneapolis, Minnesota

Harvest House Publishers has made every effort to trace the ownership of all poems and quotes. In the event of a question arising from the use of a poem or quote, we regret any error made and will be pleased to make the necessary correction in future editions of this book.

Scripture quotations are taken from The Living Bible, Copyright © 1971 owned by assignment by Illinois Regional Bank N.A. (as trustee). Used by permission of Tyndale House Publishers, Inc., Wheaton, Illinois 60189. All rights reserved; from the New American Standard Bible, © 1960, 1962, 1963, 1968, 1971, 1972, 1973, 1975, 1977 by The Lockman Foundation. Used by permission; from the Holy Bible, New International Version®, Copyright © 1973, 1978, 1984 by the International Bible Society. Used by permission of Zondervan Publishing House; from the New King James Version, Copyright © 1979, 1980, 1982 by Thomas Nelson, Inc., Publishers. Used by permission; and from the Revised Standard Version of the Bible, Copyright 1946, 1952, 1971, by the Division of Christian Education of the National Council of the Churches of Christ in the U.S.A. Used by permission.

Printed in China.

99 00 01 02 03 04 05 06 07 08 /PP/ 10 9 8 7 6 5 4 3 2 1

By wisdom a house is built, and through understanding
it is established; through knowledge its
rooms are filled with rare and beautiful treasures.

THE BOOK OF PROVERBS

The memory of home and you,
dear girls, will keep me safe.

LOUISA MAY ALCOTT

… yet the old house, the room, the merry voices and smiling faces, the jest, the laugh, the most minute and trivial circumstances connected with those happy meetings, crowd upon our mind as if the last assemblage had been but yesterday.

CHARLES DICKENS

5

There is nothing more noble or more admirable than when
two people who see eye to eye keep house as man and wife,
confounding their enemies and delighting their friends.

HOMER

6

Aunt Em had just come out of the
house to water the cabbages when
she looked up and saw Dorothy
running toward her.
"My darling child!" she cried,
folding the little girl in her arms and
covering her face with kisses,
"where in the world have you
come from?"
"From the Land of Oz," said
Dorothy gravely. "And here is Toto,
too. And oh, Aunt Em! I'm so glad
to be at home again!"

L. FRANK BAUM

The wisdom that comes
from heaven is
first of all pure and full
of quiet gentleness.

THE BOOK OF JAMES

Peace be to this house.

THE BOOK OF LUKE

8

Love…binds everything together
in perfect harmony.

THE BOOK OF COLOSSIANS

Ah! There is nothing like
staying home, for real comfort.

JANE AUSTEN

9

Home is where
one starts from.
T.S. ELIOT

Peace, like charity,
begins at home.
FRANKLIN D. ROOSEVELT

10

Home is the one place in
all the world where hearts
are sure of each other.

FREDERICK W. ROBERTSON

What Is a Home?

It is the laughter of a child,
The song of a mother
The strength of a father
Home is the first school
And the first church where
They learn about a loving God.

EDGAR A. GUEST

The beauty of the home is order;
The blessing of the home is contentment;
The glory of the home is hospitality;
The crown of the home is godliness.

AUTHOR UNKNOWN

13

The original twelve boys had of course scattered far and wide
during these years, but all that lived still remembered
Plumfield, and came wandering back from the four quarters of
the earth to tell their various experiences, laugh over the
pleasures of the past, and face the duties of the present with
fresh courage; for such home-comings keep hearts tender and
hands helpful with the memories of young and happy days.

LOUISA MAY ALCOTT

Here's to our Home—the only
spot on earth where the faults and
failings of fallen humanity are
hidden under a mantle of charity.

AUTHOR UNKNOWN

15

The Lord bless you and keep you; The Lord make His face to shine on you

A little house well filled, a little field well tilled,
and a little wife well willed, are great riches.

POOR RICHARD'S ALMANAC

be gracious to you; The Lord lift up His countenance on you; And give you peace.

Numbers 6:24-26

It was good to think he had this to come back to, this place which was all his own, these things which were so glad to see him again and could always be counted upon for the same simple welcome.

KENNETH GRAHAME

17

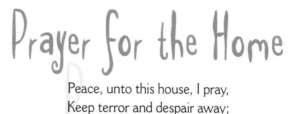

Prayer for the Home

Peace, unto this house, I pray,
Keep terror and despair away;
Shield it from evil and let sin
Never find lodging room within.
May never in these walls be heard
The hateful or accusing word.

Grant that its warm and mellow light
May be to all a beacon bright,
A flaming symbol that shall stir
The beating pulse of him or her
Who finds this door and seems to say,
"Here end the trials of the day."

18

Hold us together, gentle Lord,
Who sit about this humble board;
May we be spared the cruel fate
Of those whom hatreds separate;
Here let love bind us fast, that we
May know the joys of unity.

Lord, this humble house we'd keep
Sweet with play and calm with sleep.
Help us so that we may give
Beauty to the lives we live.
Let Thy love and let Thy grace
Shine upon our dwelling place.

EDGAR A. GUEST

19

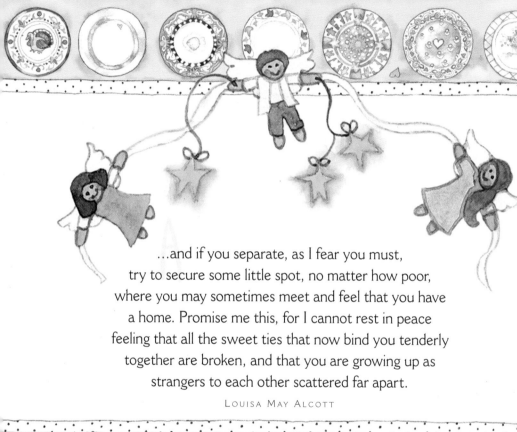

...and if you separate, as I fear you must,
try to secure some little spot, no matter how poor,
where you may sometimes meet and feel that you have
a home. Promise me this, for I cannot rest in peace
feeling that all the sweet ties that now bind you tenderly
together are broken, and that you are growing up as
strangers to each other scattered far apart.

LOUISA MAY ALCOTT

I pray Heaven to bestow the best of blessings on this house and all that shall hereinafter inhabit it. May none but honest and wise men ever rule under this roof.

LETTER TO ABIGAIL ADAMS

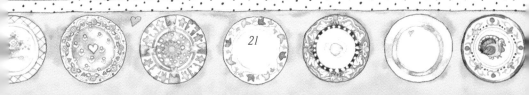

The house of everyone is to him as his castle and fortress, as well for his defense against injury and violence as for his repose.

SIR EDWARD COKES

The house shows the owner.

GEORGE HERBERT

But after the evening talk was done, the evening song sung,
and the house grew still with beautiful Sunday silence, Dan lay
in his pleasant room wide awake, thinking new thoughts,
feeling new hopes and desires stirring in his boyish heart, for
two good angels had entered in: love and gratitude.

LOUISA MAY ALCOTT

A man's house is
his best refuge.

AUTHOR UNKNOWN

Peace be to you, and
peace be to your
house, and peace be
to all that you have.

THE BOOK OF 1 SAMUEL

... and to him who knocks
the door will be opened.

Matthew 7:8

24

When I was home, I was in a better place.

WILLIAM SHAKESPEARE

Sweet is the smile of home; the mutual look,
    When hearts are of each other sure.

JOHN KEBLE

In happy homes he saw the light
Of household fires gleam warm and bright.

HENRY WADSWORTH LONGFELLOW

26

Every bird likes its own nest best.

RANDLE COTGRAVE

The Path That Leads to Home

The little path that leads to home,
That is the road for me,
I know no finer path to roam
With finer sights to see.
With thoroughfares the world is lined
That lead to wonders new,
But he who treads them leaves behind
The tender and the true.

Oh, north and south and east and west
    The crowded roadways go,
And sweating brow and weary breast
    Are all they seem to know.
And mad for pleasure some are bent,
    And some are seeking fame,
And some are sick with discontent,
    And some are bruised and lame.

Across the world the gleaming steel
    Holds out its lure for men,
But no one finds his comfort real
    Till he comes home again.
And charted lanes now line the sea
    For weary hearts to roam,
But, oh, the finest path to me
    Is that which leads to home.

'Tis there I come to laughing eyes
    And find a welcome true;
'Tis there all care behind me lies
    And joy is ever new.
And, oh, when every day is done
    Upon that little street,
A pair of rosy youngsters run
    To me with flying feet.

The world with myriad paths is lined
    but one alone for me,
One little road where I may find
    The charms I want to see.
Though thoroughfares majestic call
    The multitudes to roam,
I would not leave, to know them all,
    The path that leads to home.

EDGAR A. GUEST

One's home is the safest refuge to everyone.

SIR EDWARD COKES

I will lie down and sleep in peace, for you alone,
O Lord, make me dwell in safety.

THE BOOK OF PSALMS

East or west, home is best.

H.G. BOHN

The sun shines warmer at home.

ALBANIAN PROVERB

31

I read within a poet's book
A word that starred the page,
"Stone walls do not a prison make,
Nor iron bars a cage."
Yes, that is true, and something more:
You'll find, where're you roam,
That marble floors and gilded walls
Can never make a home.
But every house where Love abides
And Friendship is a guest,
Is surely home, and home, sweet home,
For there the heart can rest.

HENRY VAN DYKE

It is very difficult to understand anybody without
visiting his home. Houses reveal character.

GILBERT HIGHET

Make two homes for thyself, my daughter. One
actual home…and another spiritual home, which
thou art to carry with thee always.

LETTER TO MONNA ALESSA DEI SARACINI,
ST. CATHERINE OF SIENA

33

Keep the home fire burning,
While your hearts are yearning,
Though your lads are far away
They dream of home.

LENA GUILBERT FORD

Where we love is home, Home that our
feet may leave, but not our hearts.

OLIVER WENDELL HOLMES

34

Stay, stay at home, my heart, and rest;
Home-keeping hearts are happiest,
For those that wander they know not where
Are full of trouble and full of care;
To stay at home is best.

HENRY WADSWORTH LONGFELLOW

By the fireside still the light is shining,
The children's arms round the parents twining.
From love so sweet, O who would roam?
Be it ever so homely, home is home.

D.M. MULOCK

Home is the resort
Of love, of joy, of peace, and plenty; where
Supporting and supported, polished friends
And dear relations mingle into bliss.

THOMSON

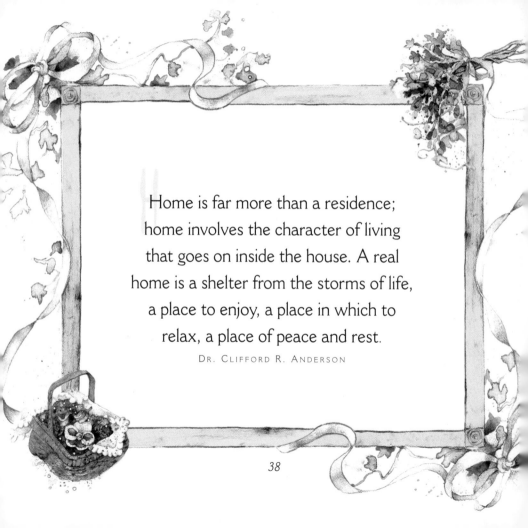

Home is far more than a residence;
home involves the character of living
that goes on inside the house. A real
home is a shelter from the storms of life,
a place to enjoy, a place in which to
relax, a place of peace and rest.

DR. CLIFFORD R. ANDERSON

38

The strength or weakness of our country lies in the homes because the home is the beginning point of everything. Honesty begins at home. Respect for law and order begins at home. Love begins at home. A sense of duty begins at home. Respect for people of other colors and creeds begins at home. And religion has its first beginning in the home.

T. CECIL MYERS

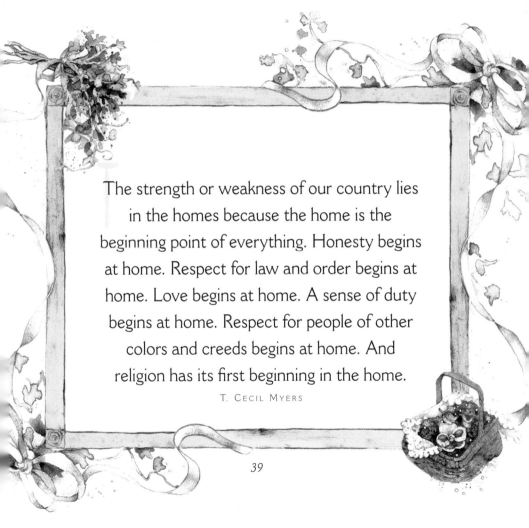

A home without laughter is a home without love.

J. GORDON

A house without love may be a castle, or a palace,
but it is not a home; love is the life of a true home.

JOHN LUBBOCK

40

Dark is the night, and fitful and drearily
Rushes the wind, like the waves of the sea!
Little care I, as here I sit cheerily,
Wife at my side and my baby on my knee:
King, king, crown me king:
Home is the kingdom and love is the king!

WILLIAM RANKIN DURYEA

Home is the place to do the things you want to do.

ZELDA FITZGERALD

It takes a hundred men to make an encampment,
but one woman can make a home.

ROBERT G. INGERSOLL

I have been very happy with my homes, but homes really
are no more than the people who live in them.

NANCY REAGAN

Home, in one form or another, is the great object in life.

J.G. HOLLAND

Old home! Old hearts! Upon my soul forever
Their peace and gladness lie like tears and laughter.

MADISON CAWEIN

No place is more delightful than one's own fireside.

AUTHOR UNKNOWN

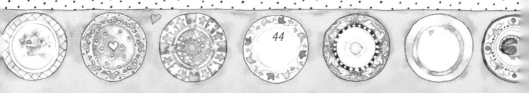

44

Home Is Where
There Is One to Love Us

Home's not merely four square walls,
Though with pictures hung and gilded;
Home is where Affection calls—
Filled with shrines the Hearth had builded!
Home! Go watch the faithful dove,
Sailing 'neath the heaven above us.
Home is where there's one to love!
Home is where there's one to love us.

Home's not merely roof and room,
It needs something to endear it;
Home is where the heart can bloom,
Where there's some kind lip to cheer it!
What is home with none to meet,
None to welcome, none to greet us?
Home is sweet, and only sweet,
Where there's one we love to meet us!

CHARLES SWAIN

Blest be that spot, where cheerful guests retire
To pause from toil, and trim their ev'ning fire;
Blest that abode, where want and pain repair,
And every stranger finds a ready chair.

OLIVER GOLDSMITH

A comfortable house is a great source
of happiness. It ranks immediately after
health and a good conscience.

SYDNEY SMITH, LETTER TO LORD MURRAY

To be happy at home is the ultimate
result of all ambition.

SAMUEL JOHNSON

47

'Tis joy to him that toils, when toil is o'er,
To find home waiting, full of happy things.

EURIPIDES

God looks down well pleased to mark
In earth's dusk each rosy spark,
Lights of home and lights of love,
And the child the heart thereof.

KATHERINE TYNAN

There's no place like home, and many a man is glad for it.

F.M. KNOWLES

Home—a world of strife shut out,
a world of love shut in.
Home—a place where the small are great,
and the great are small.
Home—the father's kingdom, the mother's world,
and the child's paradise.
Home—the place where we grumble the most,
and are treated the best.
Home—the center of our affection, round which our
heart's best wishes twine.
Home—the place where our stomachs get three
square meals a day and our hearts a thousand.

CHARLES M. CROWE

How wonderful it is, how pleasant,
when brothers live in harmony!

THE BOOK OF PSALMS

A house was never taken good care of,
Mr. Shepherd observed, without a lady…

JANE AUSTEN

51

"I don't know yet what it is, or where it will be in reality, but I have a little house o' dreams all furnished in my imagination…"

L.M. MONTGOMERY

I remember, I remember
The house where I was born,
The little window where the sun
Came peeping in at morn.

THOMAS HOOD

There is no reason either in prose or in rhyme,
why a whole house should not be a poem.

ELLA CHURCH REDMAN

Govern a family as you would cook
a small fish—very gently.

PROVERB

You will find, as you look back upon your life, that the moments that stand out, the moments when you have really lived, are the moments when you have done things in the spirit of love.

HENRY DRUMMOND

This is really the jolliest little place I ever was in. Now, wherever did you pick up those prints? Make the place look so home-like, they do. No wonder you're so fond of it, Mole. Tell us all about it, and how you came to make it what it is.

KENNETH GRAHAME
THE WIND IN THE WILLOWS

Eliza slept and dreamed of peace,
Of lands where all is rest;
Of bright, green shores where sorrows cease,
Of homes which God had blest.

ELOISE A. BABB

56

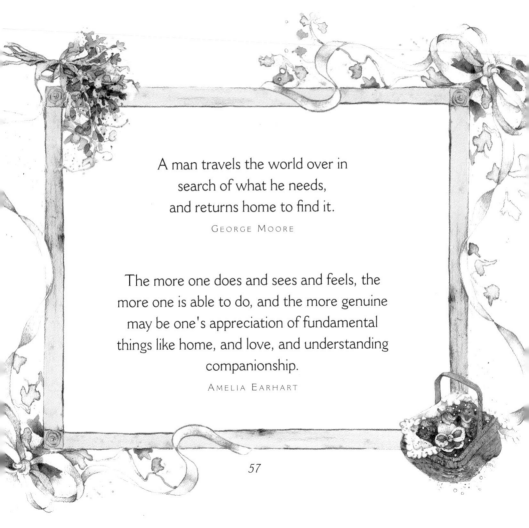

A man travels the world over in
search of what he needs,
and returns home to find it.

GEORGE MOORE

The more one does and sees and feels, the
more one is able to do, and the more genuine
may be one's appreciation of fundamental
things like home, and love, and understanding
companionship.

AMELIA EARHART

This is the true nature of home—it is the
place of Peace; the shelter, not only from injury,
but from all terror, doubt and division.

JOHN RUSKIN

The family is the school of duties... founded on love.

FELIX ADLER

58

You leave home to seek your fortune and, when you get it,
you go home and share it with your family.

ANITA BAKER

Nor need we power or splendor, wide hall or lordly dome; the
good, the true, the tender—these form the wealth of home.

SARAH J. HALE

Call it a clan, call it a network, call it a tribe,
call it a family: Whatever you call it,
whoever you are, you need one.

JANE HOWARD

A family is a place where principles
are hammered and honed on the
anvil of everyday living.

CHARLES SWINDOLL

The ornament
of a house is
the friends
who frequent it.

<small>RALPH WALDO EMERSON</small>

61

A close-knit and loving home is
worth more than a kingdom.

WILLIAM BENNETT

They came around the corner, and there was
Eeyore's house, looking as comfy as anything.

A.A. MILNE
The House at Pooh Corner

62

Nat saw a large square house before him—a hospitable-looking house, with an old-fashioned porch, wide steps, and lights shining in many windows. Neither curtains nor shutters hid the cheerful glimmer; and, pausing a moment before he rang, Nat saw many little shadows dancing on the walls, heard the pleasant hum of young voices, and felt that it was hardly possible that the light and warmth and comfort within could be for a homeless "little chap" like him.

LOUISA MAY ALCOTT

There it was! It looked so small, like a one-car garage.
Yet in my heart I saw a home, bigger than life, with
Mama's cookstove and rocking chair in it…. I could
almost hear the squeak of the rocker, and I marveled
at how five children had lived here and found ample
room in Mama's lap. From that rocker we learned our
theology, big lessons of faith in a tiny house.

MARGARET JENSEN